TEEN LEADERSHIP UNLOCKED

Teen's Empowerment Essentials:
Unlocking the Secrets to Effective Leadership

by

Stan Willson

© **Copyright 2024 by Stan Willson. All rights reserved.**

No portion of this publication may be kept in a retrieval system, copied, or shared in any form or medium, digital, scanning, recording, printing, mechanical, or otherwise, Without the prior written permission of the Publisher unless authorized explicitly by 1976 United States Copyright Act, section 107 or 108. Contact the Publisher's permission department with any questions about permission.

Legal Notice

This book is covered by copyright. It is only to be utilized personally. No one can rephrase, quote, copy, distribute, sell, or change any part of the details in this book without the author's or Publisher's permission.

Disclaimer Notice

This book is composed and published independently. Please bear in mind that the content in this resource is solely for educational and entertaining purposes. All information has been given accurately, up-to-date, reliable, and comprehensively. Neither explicit nor implicit guarantees are made. This book's content aims to oblige readers to understand the subject matter better. The activities, data, and exercises are provided solely for self-help knowledge. This book is not intended to supersede expert psychologists or legal, financial, or other guidance. If you instruct counseling, please consider and communicate with a qualified professional.

By reading this content, the reader takes that the author will not be held accountable for any damages, directly or indirectly, due to the application of the information included herein, mainly, but not restricted to, omissions, errors, or inaccuracies. You are liable for your decisions, actions, and consequences as a reader.

Author Bio

Stan Willson is an author and specialist in self-mastery for youth. With a profound knowledge of adolescent challenges, Tyler provides practical approaches and guidance to help teens develop essential skills to become influential leaders and navigate their leadership journey. Through his exquisite and informative self-help books, he offers valuable insights and practical advice on various aspects of leadership.

Table of Content

SOME THOUGHTS 08

INTRODUCTION 09

PART 1: FUNDAMENTALS OF LEADERSHIP 12

SOW THE SEEDS OF THE LEADERSHIP JOURNEY 12

Different Leadership Styles 13

1. Autocratic Leadership 13

2. Laissez-faire Leadership 13

3. Democratic Leadership 13

4. Bureaucratic Leadership 14

Twelve Leadership Qualities 16

Leadership Building Activities 19

1. Minefield 19

2. Lego Building 19

3. Team Volunteering 19

4. Bingo 20

5. Get Off The Settee 20

6. Snack Challenge 20

7. Marshmallow Tower 20

8. Participation 21

9. Sports 21

10. The One-minute Story Challenge 22

Leadership Problems.. 23

Discover Teen Leadership Potential... 25

Real-life Story: Zuriel Oduwole... 26

A Diversity of Roles In Leadership.. 27

Significance of Leadership Roles.. 27

Examples of Leadership Roles.. 28

1. Manager.. 28

2. Mentor.. 28

3. Trainer.. 28

4. Organizer.. 29

5. Coach... 29

Difference Between Team And Individual Leadership Types... 30

Real-life Story: Isra Hirsi.. 31

Key Takeaways.. 32

Thinking Time... 33

PART 2: THE IMPORTANT CORNERSTONE........................ 34

IMPORTANT LEADERSHIP CORNERSTONES..................... 34

KEY LEADERSHIP VALUES... 36

1. Service.. 36

2. Passion... 36

3. Vision... 36

List of Leadership Values.. 37

How to Nurture Leadership Values.. 38

1. Choose Your Leadership Style.. 38

2. Examine Your Decisions.. 38

3. Reflect On Experiences.. 38

4. Create A Values List... 39

5. Apply Your Leadership Values... 39

Understanding Leadership Communication............................. 40

Eleven Leadership's Principles.. 46

Public Speaking Tips... 48

Real-life Story: Greta Thunberg... 51

Key Takeaways... 52

Thinking Time... 53

PART 3: APPROACHES AND METHODS FOR TEEN LEADERS.. 54

SETTING GOALS AND TIME MANAGEMENT.................... 54

Balancing Studies And Leadership... 60

Do Not Delay Things... 63

Real-life Story: Jahkil Jackson.. 65

Formulating And Leading Effective Teams................................ 66

Team-building Activities.. 69

Real-life Story: Jaylen Arnold... 70

Key Takeaways... 71

Thinking Time... 72

PART 4: REAL-LIFE APPLICATIONS AND IMPACT............ 73

CREATING A GLOBAL IMPACT.. 73

The Ever-changing Nature of The Contemporary Workplace.. 74

Embracing Diversity, Fairness, And Inclusion............................ 74

Lack of Experience.. 74

Social Pressure.. 74

Presenting Innovative Concepts And Perspectives..................... 75

Digital Proficiency.. 75

Influencing Public Policy... 75

Real-life Story: Gitanjali Rao... 79

Key Takeaways.. 80

Thinking Time.. 81

MEET THE LEADERSHIP INSPO... 82

CONCLUSION... 84

Some Thoughts

> *"A leader knows the path, goes the path and shows the path."*
> J. C. Maxwell

The best time to start learning how to be a leader is when you are young! You can find leadership lessons everywhere in your daily life. Dear teen, leaders are not born. They are ordinary people with extraordinary skills. They refine their skills and attributes and work hard to become great aspiring leaders.

Being a young leader is a journey that helps you grow and change, along with the people and community around you. A leader has many roles and skills, like setting goals, communication, making decisions, and more.

This book will help you become a strong teen leader. It will provide you with tips and tools to be prepared and succeed in your leadership role.

Introduction

"Leadership is the ability to crack a vision into actuality."
W.Bennis

Do you know? Becoming a great leader takes time and hard work. Being a good leader means always learning from your studies, life experiences, and trying new things like, pushing yourself beyond your limits and thinking about new ideas.

All leaders have something in common, they all have good values. They are honest, caring, and thoughtful. They stand up for what they believe in, even if they are alone and have no support. They are kind and understanding. They listen to others, respect different cultures, and are open to new ideas.

Dear teen, leaders must understand people before helping and guiding them. The best way to understand others is to grow empathy inside you. It is an ability to understand how someone feels, and it is an important skill for every leader.

Always remember that good leaders lead by example. They set goals and they work hard to achieve them. And instead of giving up after defeat, they learn from failures and mistakes and become stronger than before.

Leadership might seem difficult to keep up with sometimes, but it is a process that keeps on growing you into the most amazing version of yourself. Leaders lead others, showing them a clear vision, a path in front of them to reach. They are a source of motivation and inspiration to everyone around them. They continuously help their teams to adjust to new situations and become strong.

A leader is not just a boss bossing around and ordering everyone. It's more than just that. It's taking everyone ahead with yourself rather than going to the top alone. Great leaders are confident, dependable, and honest.

The world is changing rapidly and there are new situations for you to tackle each day. In such a time, to be a leader you must know how to plan solutions for tough problems. You should also know how to use new tech and handle new situations. You need to learn to appreciate others' ideas and grow together by understanding what your team needs to be successful.

You cannot become a leader by swishing a magic wand or saying a magic spell. It might not be a piece of cake like that but it's a skill that makes you feel important and gets better with practice. And trust yourself; if you start developing this skill in yourself from teenage, till adulthood, you will already become a great leader.

True leaders go ahead with a clear plan. They don't just go with the flow, they make their path! They care for people around them and keep the team together. You must take responsibility for your actions as a good leader.

So, dear teen! This book will take you on a ride to leadership. It will include several tips and inspiring real-life stories that will make becoming a leader all the more fun for you! You will learn that leadership is not just about having a special title or position. It is something you can do at any level and in many parts of your life. Leadership is about positively influencing and guiding others toward a common goal, whether it is in a job, a community project, or in your personal life.

Part 1
FUNDAMENTALS OF LEADERSHIP

Sow the Seeds of the Leadership Journey

> *"Management is carrying out things right; leadership is carrying out the right things."*

Leadership is about getting others to follow you. A person who can do this has leadership qualities and is a perfect fit to be a leader. Leadership can look different depending on the person, culture, and situation, but it is always a challenging role and requires a special skillset.

Good leadership is constructive and helps the team grow. It sets goals, creates a vision, and allows for flexibility when needed. Leadership is about doing what is needed to succeed as a team. It is exciting and inspiring. In this section, we will learn about different leadership styles, roles, responsibilities, and the qualities of a good leader.

Different Leadership Styles

Dear teen, you must be thinking! You might notice many leaders around you, each with a unique way of leading. There must be different types of leadership styles. Yes, you are correct. There are various types of leadership, and all leaders have a different style that sets them apart. Let's explore different leadership styles that will guide you to choose which type of leader you want to be and what skills you need to have.

1. Autocratic Leadership

A leader with complete control over his team is named an autocratic leader. Such a leader never changes his views and practices for anyone. The team of such a leader has no say in decision-making. Moreover, the team is expected to follow the commands of the leader without any question.

This old-fashioned leadership style has very limited followers because change is not welcomed here.

2. Laissez-Faire Leadership

"Laissez-faire" is a French term meaning "let them do." In this style, team members do their tasks as they choose. They can share their ideas and use their skills without the leader telling them exactly what to do. This allows team members to be creative and work in a way that suits them best.

3. Democratic Leadership

In this style, the leader and the team work together to achieve goals. Similarly, they work together and motivate each other on personal and professional grounds. It is a positive style that creates a good working environment.

4. Bureaucratic Leadership

Bureaucratic leaders strictly follow rules and expect the same from their team. They are usually very organized and driven.

As a teen, it is important to understand that there are no strictly good or bad leadership styles, it is your choice what kind of leader you want to be.

Qualities of a Good Leader:

- **Communication**

Good leaders use effective communication. Communication is the tool that helps leaders develop trust within their teams and set responsibilities to achieve the goals. Leaders should communicate about rewards and consequences to keep the team committed. A good leader listens and understands team members' struggles. Regular communication resolves disputes, tracks progress, and builds trust.

- **Foresighted and Strategic Thinking**

Influential leaders can outline a vision for their goal that motivates and channels their team members' energies toward the same goal. Just setting a big picture of your goals is not enough, a good leader should come up with an effective strategy that will guide the whole team. The leader should provide a roadmap that should include all aspects that influence the goals and perspectives of team members. This will make team members feel that they are directly involved in the success of goals.

- **Empowerment**

Good leaders do not micromanage. They give team members the tools, skills, and knowledge to succeed on their own. Eventually, good leaders know that their success is connected to every team member. A good leader lets the team work on their own independently without having a constant watch over them.

In addition to ensuring the overall team's success, leaders also develop the unique skills of each team member by empowering them. By empowering the team, leaders encourage new ideas and creative solutions.

- **Adaptability**

Change is constant. Leaders must adapt to new trends, technologies, and expectations. This means welcoming new disciplines, technologies or expectations. Adaptability is the trait that enables leaders to see change as an opportunity, which makes their goals more flexible, efficient, and simpler to achieve success.

- **Self-Awareness**

Leaders need self-awareness to grow. They should regularly seek feedback to understand their weaknesses and improve. Self-awareness helps leaders learn from their failures and avoid making the same mistakes. Self-awareness also allows leaders to evaluate their failures openly, enabling them to see what went wrong and take action to avoid similar errors in the future.

Leadership is an essential skill for teens to develop. While you will continue to improve your leadership style through school and future jobs, it is good to understand what makes a great leader and what prevents a person from becoming one.

I have compiled a list of twelve leadership qualities, ten leadership-building activities and ten leadership challenges to guide your understanding of leadership. They will help you become a better leader in the future.

Twelve Leadership Qualities

Given below are the 12 leadership qualities.

1. Bravery

Bravery is the courage to keep going, especially in uncertain or challenging times. It involves making tough decisions that benefit others, even if those decisions cause you to be disliked temporarily. Leaders who demonstrate bravery inspire confidence and trust among their colleagues and followers alike.

2. Self-Control

Self-control is the ability to manage your emotions, behaviors, and impulses, particularly in stressful or difficult situations. Leaders with strong self-control are admired for their ability to remain calm under pressure and make reasoned decisions. They are a role model for others too as they handle difficulties calmly with good spirits and flexibility.

3. Fairness

Fairness in leadership is the act of understanding everyone's needs and interests without bias. You must actively listen to everyone's viewpoints and make decisions after that. Your decisions should focus on achieving the outcomes that will be mutually beneficial for the majority. Fair leaders promote fairness and build trust among team members.

4. Preparation

One of the biggest qualities that make leaders different from others is that they prepare themselves before action. They design strategies, make plans, and then move towards their goal. They keep some portion for flexibility in case of changing situations. Preparation makes you and your teammates feel confident because you have clarity about your plan.

5. Taking the Extra Step

Leaders hold the responsibility to take their teams forward. So they take the initiative. They look for opportunities and achieve beyond minimum requirements. By taking the extra step leaders bring motivation and commitment to their teams.

6. Appealing Personality

Good leaders are kind, approachable, and respectful. They understand the emotions and opinions of others. They are supportive and create a friendly environment, making everyone feel understood and valued. Good leaders avoid rudeness and sarcasm.

7. Kindness and Understanding

It might seem hard for others to understand everyone's perspective but not for a leader. A good leader is kind, talks with politeness and respects everyone. A kind leader shows care and understanding, making a strong team built on mutual support.

8. Detail Oriented

Detail oriented means paying close attention. When a good leader pays more attention to details throughout the decision-making process, he reduce the chances of mistakes and failures. Detail orientation is also called meticulousness. This quality really helps in enhancing performance and quality, since you get saved from tiny mistakes leading to big failures.

9. Sense of Accountability

Accountability is the willingness to take responsibility for your actions and decisions. Good leaders are truthful, acknowledge their mistakes, learn from failures, and share the credit of success with their teams.

10. Collaboration

Collaboration is the ability to work effectively with others. Leaders know that the teams are made to achieve a shared objective and goal. So they encourage everyone to talk and help each other.

11. Integrity

Integrity means the consistency between your words, actions, and values. It means, being the same from inside and outside. Good leaders don't fake, don't lie, and don't promote dishonesty. They build trust by staying honest, fair, and devoted to the team.

12. Honesty

There might come times when there will be hard news to deliver to the team, but a good leader always says what's right. They are honest and promote transparency between the team members. Such qualities build strong relationships between the teams and their leaders.

Leadership Building Activities

Games for making a team grow stronger are also a helpful and fun practice to follow, and they help in developing leadership skills too. Such games help in learning how to work together to achieve a common goal. Below are some of the fun activities and ideas you can follow to develop leadership and a good bond with your team.

1. Minefield

Minefield is the activity that focuses on better communication and trust-building between team members. In this activity, you give clear instructions and guide your blindfolded teammates over a fake minefield. This activity emphasizes the importance of good communication and active listening in teamwork.

2. Lego Building

Lego building exercise makes you learn how to work in teams with creativity. It also promotes problem-solving by considering others' ideas. Team members work together towards a common goal while building structures using Lego bricks.

3. Team Volunteering

Volunteering helps develop a crucial leadership skill: assertiveness. Also, volunteering to help others allows you to build connections and a good personality. You also build trust in your team and in yourself, making it easier to achieve various goals. Engaging in community service is one of the most influential leadership activities of today and it is the core of every structured leadership program.

4. Bingo

Community bingo is a helpful way to better understand the leaders in a community, and their various leadership roles and styles. The objective is to meet with community leaders and learn about their roles or styles. Participants engage with leaders from various backgrounds, learning about their experiences and leadership approaches in an interactive and enjoyable setting

5. Get off the Settee

The "Get off the Settee" activity explores motivational strategies and individual motivations. Participants identify what motivates themselves and others, practicing empathy and learning how to inspire and support team members towards achieving collective goals.

6. Snack Challenge

The "Tag Team Snack Challenge" is a quick game which highlights non-verbal communication and its importance. Each participant takes as a leader and leaves hints for the next participant as they work hand-in-hand to complete a specified snack at a designated time. This game polishes your time management skills and helps you think out of the box.

7. Marshmallow Tower

This is a game you play with marshmallow and spaghetti. Yes! You and your team would have to build the tallest tower in 18 minutes with the help of 20 sticks of spaghetti, one marshmallow, one meter of tape, one meter of string or yard, and one marshmallow. This game helps the team polish their communication and group work skills.

8. Participation

What could be more beneficial than getting firsthand experience of leadership? For this, you should participate in situations which require you to collaborate with others. School clubs and communities can be a good place to start. Through such participation, your decision-making and problem-solving skills are polished. You also learn to communicate with people in a better way.

So, avail all the chances to become part of extracurricular activities. You can organize a book fair, run a one-week challenge for different causes, or maybe plan a historical play with your classmates. These activities will allow you to meet new people and learn from them.

9. Sports

We all love to play in our teen years because that puts the energy in our body to good use. So why don't you participate in some team sports to have some fun besides polishing your leadership potential? Sports make you able to work as a team which is the crux of leadership.

You work together on a common goal and make plans to achieve it. But you don't just have to play to succeed, you can win only because of teamwork and hard work. You can become good at communication and adapt to different situations through playing sports in the form of teams.

10. The One-Minute Story Challenge

Since childhood, you've been listening to stories. This doesn't stop when you grow up. Everyone wants to listen to a good story no matter their age. Can you tell a story in one minute? I hope you can. This is going to be fun for you. To do this you have to create a unique story in 1 minute with a scenario provided to you. The player with the most claps is the winner in this game. This is all fun and creative! This will polish your team bonding and creative skills.

These activities will not only develop your leadership qualities but also affect your studies, job, and personal growth because you'll learn some good communication, teamwork, and problem-solving skills.

Leadership Problems

1. Reluctance to Provide Low-Key Service

Becoming a leader isn't an easy role when it comes to dealing with others. There might be times when you as a leader have to do the tasks of others or maybe you have to do things which no one else is determined to do. It takes guts to be someone who can bring a good and easy solution to a very tough situation.

2. Reluctance to Document One's Work

A genuine leader empowers others by offering them an opportunity to document their mistakes and successes. It is essential to take the time to document what is working and what is not.

3. Fear of Contest

Leaders who fear others will likely be leaders for a short time. A leader's goal is to empower others. A person's value is increased if they can mentor and facilitate other leaders.

4. Lack of Imagination

A leader needs creativity and vision to effectively deal with problems. Even small improvements in daily tasks can lead to big changes, and leaders encourage this in others. Leaders are people who promote this approach in others.

5. Narcissism

A strong leader gives credit and takes responsibility. Not acknowledging others' efforts leads to resentment. Of course, someone who consistently refuses to give credit to the efforts of others will be disliked.

6. Poor Discipline in Personal Life

Some leaders often fail due to a lack of discipline in their personal lives. To look fit and be prosperous, it is a must to exercise, nurture connections, and avoid indecent relationships.

7. Betrayal

Trust is vital for a leader. Leaders must be trustworthy to earn loyalty from their team.

8. Being Inflexible

Leaders who are too rigid do not last long. However, the best leaders are role models, who encourage combined development and engage in negotiation with their team. It provides them with future benefits and this style of leadership wins in the long run.

9. Insisting on Being Correct

Leaders who often consider their stand as the "right thing" keep a biased approach. Leaders who always think they are right create conflict. Good leaders seek fairness and compromise.

10. Ignorance of the Totality

Several leaders stumbled when motivated by a single goal, like when a company leader makes judgments solely on profit. The finest leaders make decisions based on the influence of those who may have a direct effect on the decision and also those who may be indirectly impacted.

With these guiding principles, you will be on the trail toward becoming an optimistic and prosperous leader in your life's endeavors.

Discover Teen Leadership Potential

When we hear or think of present-day icons, we usually link them with the important changes they made in their adult years. Yet, today's youth can also bring changes and some are already making a worldwide positive impact. This resource contains some of the most influential teen leaders who changed the world and inspired us.

Real-Life Story: Zuriel Oduwole

Zuriel Oduwole, a Los Angeles native, is renowned for her global development work, advocating for female education across the African and Caribbean regions. At age 10, in 2013, she was portrayed in Forbes Magazine and listed among 33 women who had transformed the world by ELLE Magazine in 2015. In January 2017, she was named the world's most powerful girl. The US Secretary of State honored her in Washington DC at the State Department for her enthusiastic work advocating against budding marriage and girls' education. Zuriel had one-on-one meetings with more than 30 Presidents and Prime Ministers to address youths' global social development and education challenges.

A Diversity of Roles in Leadership

Dear teens, leaders are responsible for leading, managing and directing; they are forward-thinkers and influencers and they motivate their fellows toward accomplishing their expected goals.

Significance of Leadership Roles

Leaders guide their teams and fellows toward attaining goals and achieving positive results in a contemporary work setting. The challenges posed by developing technologies, flexible work environments, and political uncertainty demand leaders who can efficiently handle them.

Leadership roles are crucial to the success of any team or organization. Following are some fundamental reasons why leadership roles are essential:

- Encouraging and motivating fellows to perform towards common goals and facilitating them to perform their best.
- Delivering transparent guidance to the fellows and teams, establishing goals and objectives, and clarifying the path to success.
- Making critical decisions that can influence the success of the team and the organization.
- Communicating their notion to the team and fostering open and direct communication to make sure that all members are on the same page.
- Bearing ownership and responsibility for the success and setbacks of their teams.
- Adapting to changing factors and challenges and ensuring the team stays determined and on the path toward their goals.

Examples of Leadership Roles

Following are various roles to consider if you want to be a leader:

1. Manager

Managers play a crucial role in organizations by guiding and organizing teams. They provide direction, supervise tasks, and ensure everyone is working together towards the same goals. Managers are responsible for the overall performance of their team and the success of projects.

2. Mentor

People often pursue their mentors for advice and guidance on performing in their workplace due to their extensive knowledge, expertise and background. As a mentor, you must be prepared to offer practical information when required and can give examples from your past experiences to shape your mentees' careers. Mentors have years of vigorous experience, guidance and advice that can help their mentees both in the present and the future.

3. Trainer

Leaders sometimes perform the trainer's role to familiarize people with the fundamental means and work procedures. A trainer may help others understand their roles, suggest appropriate courses to enhance their skills and knowledge and organize workshops to improve their productivity. This role demands the patience to instruct fellows when they repeatedly make blunders and the wisdom to know how to address those mistakes effectively.

4. Organizer

Logical thinking, strategic planning, effective communication, event management, and efficient task completion are some essential skills for a leader. Your understanding of team functioning and projects means that you can assign tasks, establish goals, and use the variable talent effectively. The superior your leadership position, the more refined your understanding, and the more teams you may supervise and organize. Leaders who excel as organizers are skilled in planning, communication, and task management. They coordinate activities, set objectives, and ensure that each team member understands the responsibilities.

5. Coach

If you are in sports, you might have met the coach of your football or basketball team. The role of the coach in leadership is no different. A coach is someone who instructs others and trains them. A coach can make a team win because of the training, advice, and motivation he provides to the team.

Difference between Individual and Team Leadership Types

There are two types of leadership styles. Choose your style based on your strengths and weaknesses.

Individual Leadership

- **Decision-Making:** Make decisions on your own, using your insights and experiences.
- **Self-Reliance:** Depend on yourself for guidance and advice.
- **Consistency:** Stick to your views and actions.
- **Goal Setting:** Set your own goals and lead others to achieve them.
- **Potential Drawbacks:** Can limit creativity and miss out on other perspectives.

Team Leadership

- **Collaboration:** Value and seek input from team members.
- **Communication:** Encourage open communication and idea sharing.
- **Innovation:** Ask for different viewpoints to promote creativity.
- **Shared Goals:** Set goals together with your team.
- **Empowerment:** Make team members feel valued and respected.
- **Support:** Celebrate achievements and support each other through challenges.

Real-Life Story: Isra Hirsi

Isra Hirsi, a Black Muslim woman from Minneapolis, Minnesota, is a high school student who advocates for environment and racial fairness and is the co-founder and co-executive director of the "Youth Climate Strike US". Hirsi began her climate advocacy in her first year of high school by entering her environmental club.

Along with environmental justice, she participated in debate and theater at her high school. She uses her activism to enable her to not only understand the world around her but also to navigate it. As an immigrant child, Hirsi cares enormously for many issues impacting her family and community.

Hirsi has this objective to transform the world from a youngster. She has always relished helping others and ensuring every zone is friendly. She directed her passion for issues to improve the world.

> "Leadership isn't just about being in charge; it's about inspiring teamwork and cooperation to reach a shared goal."

Key Takeaways

- **Leadership Defined:** Leadership is influencing others towards a shared goal, ensuring everyone contributes effectively.

- **Leadership Styles:** Consider your natural style (directive, hands-off, collaborative, or rule-oriented) and adapt it to the situation.

- **Essential Skills:** Hone communication, strategic thinking, empowerment, adaptability, and self-awareness to be a well-rounded leader.

- **Developing Your Skills:** Actively participate in team-building activities and reflect on past leadership experiences to improve.

- **Common Mistakes:** Avoid micromanaging, unclear communication, lack of trust, and inflexibility.

- **Leadership Inspiration:** Seek out inspiring leaders like Zuriel Oduwole and Isra Hirsi.

- **Leadership Roles:** Leadership can be exercised individually or in team, through initiative and inspiration.

Thinking Time

1. What kind of leader do you want to be, and what leadership style do you like and why?
2. Have you ever shown the leadership qualities mentioned above? What did you learn from that experience?
3. Do you take part in any activities to build leadership skills? How do these activities help you personally and in your future career?
4. Have you faced any challenges as a leader? How did you handle them?
5. Why is teamwork important in leadership, and how do you plan to encourage it?

Part 2
THE LEADERSHIP FOUNDATIONS
Important Leadership Cornerstones

"Leadership builds a strong foundation of values and communication that empower people, inspire action, and shape a future where every voice carries meaning and authenticity."

The site, orientation, and resilience of a structure are defined by its cornerstone. Just as a structure requires a solid foundation to be firm, any organization also requires grounds of strength and ambition that guide its actions. These qualities usually come from its leaders and core values. But as a leader, how can you define your principles of leadership?

Understanding Leadership

Being a leader is a challenging role that requires many skills and qualities. Successful leaders have a mix of abilities, from understanding ideas and communicating well to showing empathy and being adaptable.

Leadership Cornerstones

Think of leadership like the sturdy walls of a building supported by its cornerstones. Team members look to their leader for guidance in their actions, behavior, and decisions. How a leader presents himself affects every move his team makes.

Key Leadership Values

Leadership is based on values that inspire and influence others. Here are three essential values every leader should embrace:

1. Service

Servant leadership signifies that everything you do has a purpose of helping others and making the world a better place. Those who exemplify this leadership value have found their motto in life and will not allow anything to get in their way. They aim to accomplish good in the world because they understand that it makes their life purposeful and satisfying.

2. Passion

Are you a person who wakes up every morning keen to start the day? Or are you the one who switches the snooze button and wishes for five more minutes of sleep? If waking up excited is your answer, then you have uncovered one of the most essential values of a leader. Passion drives leaders to live with energy and dedication, inspiring others to do the same.

3. Vision

Concentrate on where you like to go, not what you are afraid of. It is the essence of having a clear vision. Having a clear vision gives you confidence to stay focused, overcome challenges, and inspire others to follow your lead.

List of Leadership Values

With these above core values, renowned leaders often have other strong values that navigate their lives. The following list of leadership values can help you decide which ones you have.

- Cleverness
- Communication
- Confidence
- Dedication
- Empathy
- Flexibility
- Genuine
- Growth
- Honesty
- Humbleness
- Influence
- Innovation
- Positivity
- Toughness
- Truthfulness

How to Nurture Leadership Values

Understanding your core leadership values is key to becoming an influential leader. When you practice these values daily, you will make better decisions, inspire confidence in others, set a positive example, and motivate your team to follow you.

1. Choose Your Leadership Style

Great leadership begins with servant leadership. Your unique style combines your commitment to service with your personal values. For instance, empathetic democratic leaders prioritize empathy and communication, while visionary leaders value creativity and innovation. Affiliative leaders emphasize dedication and harmony, and pacesetting leaders focus on hard work and commitment. Once you identify your core values, you can integrate other qualities to grow as a leader.

2. Examine Your Decisions

Be mindful of the decisions you make every day. On which grounds did you make that decision? Link it back to one of your values. Reflect on the values that guide your choices. Consider which decisions were easy and which were challenging. Tough decisions may not align with your core leadership values.

3. Reflect on Experiences

Reflect on experiences beyond work. Recall the important moments when you faced strong emotions, pleasure or sadness, pride or humiliation, satisfaction or vacuum. Consider the reason behind that feeling. When you experience positive emotions, it is likely your fundamental values guide your life. Opposite to this, if you feel difficult emotions, it could be a mismatch between your values with your experience. These personal values overlay with your leadership values and provide valuable insights.

4. Create a Values List

Start by listing your leadership values. Write down each value that matters to you, then group similar ones. For example, combine genuineness, integrity, and honesty, or optimism, resilience, and adaptability. Write down every value that counts, then combine similar values to make at least five groups. This exercise helps you clarify your top five fundamental leadership values.

5. Apply Your Leadership Values

As you face new challenges and gain experience, you can consider your leadership values and use them in decision-making. If your values complement those of your work setting, you will uncover many ways to use them. However, if they do not, you can bring new insights and motivation and create a more positive and open corporate culture.

Understanding Leadership Communication

As time has progressed, leaders have come to understand the real importance of effective communication skills. Exceptional leaders continuously seek out different techniques and practices to refine and enhance their ability to communicate effectively.

The Power of Effective Communication

Let's start with understanding the position of communication skills in influential leadership.

When you think of leadership communication, do you think of great speakers like Winston Churchill or Martin Luther King Jr.? Visualize articulating to stadiums full of people or delivering TED Talks that earn millions of views. These leaders are indeed excellent public speakers, but do you know why people find them so inspiring?

Essence of Leadership Communication

Leadership and communication are the bottom lines of passion, vision and values. When you speak passionately from your heart, demonstrate emotional intelligence, and listen actively to others, you naturally inspire and engage those around you. Marc Benioff, the CEO of Salesforce, aptly summarized, "The most promising leaders are excellent communicators and listeners."

Effective communication serves as the cornerstone of leadership, playing a critical role in conflict resolution, information sharing, and building strong relationships. How to communicate effectively is a multidimensional subject. Your communication style may vary depending on whether you communicate with workers, partners, kids or strangers. In any case, it involves active listening, empathy for whom you are communicating with, body language and emotional awareness of both parties in the conversation. These elements help you deliver your message.

Enhancing Your Leadership Communication

Mastering influential communication skills can help you shift from an average to a revolutionary leader. You need to polish your communication skills. Almost all the leaders you know today can speak well.

You can polish your communication skills by using these practices:

Start With Self-Awareness

Your mind is the big game! Your team can be as successful and as strong as you can be. Do some work on yourself and understand your emotions. Think about what makes you strong and weak. When you are sure of yourself and understand yourself better, chances are high that you can lead others in a good way. When you know what you want to do and how you want to do it, you can communicate your ideas to your team effectively.

✓ Listen

You just don't have to be physically present to listen to somebody. Leadership requires active listening, which makes you actively listen to the other person and understand what is being said at the moment. You just don't want someone to listen to you and not respond. Yeah, nobody wants that.

So, a leader needs to show interest in what someone is saying. This way, your talk will also be listened to carefully by others. Active listening demands paying attention to body language, maintaining eye contact, and acknowledging the gestures.

✓ Ask Smart Questions

No one wants to be bombarded with a lot of silly questions. No one has time for that either. Asking the right questions is important for getting the right answer. A leader should ask such questions that make others think critically.

Use open-ended questions because these will help you understand the viewpoints of others. Learning to ask questions in a better way and understanding the way people talk can make you good at dealing with different situations and people.

✓ Be Honest

No one will like to follow you if you aren't honest. If you want people to be inspired by you, you should be trustworthy and honest. Say whatever there is to be said, either good or bad in a truthful way.

- Bad news shouldn't be kept from your team. They need to know it.
- Also, always tell the good news to your team as soon as you can.
- Don't complicate things and be as simple as you can be in delivering your message to others. Honest and direct leadership communication will help you meet expectations and build trust.

✓ Coordinate Your Actions

Lead by example and ensure that your actions consistently reflect your words and values. Demonstrate integrity by following through on commitments and treating others with fairness and respect. Consistency between what you say and what you do develops trust and credibility, making you a more effective and influential leader.

✓ Respond to the "Why"

Most of us don't do something blindly when asked to perform something. We naturally ask "Why?" Answering the why makes leadership communication more persuasive and influential. Always use the "because" statement with your instructions as it describes your logic and reasoning. Communicate thoughts you didn't pick and describe why not. It reveals that you've viewed alternate viewpoints and clarifies why your decision is the best choice.

✓ Narrate a Story

Stories are powerful tools for communication that can convey meaning, inspire action, and build connections. Share relevant stories or experiences that demonstrate key points and relate with your audience. Effective storytelling helps make complex ideas more relatable and memorable, capturing attention and inspiring others to action.

✓ Maestro Body Language

Teens, you may have come across the statistic that communication consists of 93% nonverbal and 7% verbal cues. While the numbers can vary, mastering body language is essential for leadership communication skills. Pay attention to your own body language and adapt it to convey confidence, empathy, and openness. Similarly, observe the body language of others to judge their reactions and better understand their perspectives. A positive and receptive body language enhances communication effectiveness and strengthens relationships. Comprehending others' body language and tone of voice also allows you to read the hidden message. What is unsaid is often actually more significant than the spoken words.

✓ Be Adaptable

Flexibility in communication styles allows you to connect with different types of audiences and deal with different situations effectively. You should have the ability to change your way of talking as per your audience. You cannot talk to your teammate and class teacher in the same manner. In the same way, you would have to switch your communication style when dealing with a best friend and your mother. The important thing it to know what to what, how to say, when to say, and to whom to say.

✓ Communicate Regularly

Leaders do not appear in their teams once in a blue moon. They also aren't some sort of a celebrity who is out of reach. An active leader keeps everyone informed of the current updates. When your team knows that you are there whenever they need to talk about something important, your team will trust you more.

Keep your team informed of your goals. Let them know about your plans and listen to their plans as well. Schedule weekly or monthly meetings for discussing matters that need combined action.

Give feedback to your team sooner than they know. Be a part of who they are and know the needs of your team. You can build a stronger connection with your team in this way.

✓ Technology Pro

This age of technology demands the availability of people beyond office hours. People communicate with each other all the time. Use technology to make things easier for your team. Know some apps or software that can help your team achieve their targets and keep track of their work.

It is important to know the fine line between online communication and maintaining your personal space. Technology cannot replace the benefit of face-to-face communication. But when needed, you can deliver your messages to your team remotely.

Allow your team to become technology professionals. Give them access to different platforms to learn and grow.

Having the ability to talk effectively is very important for becoming an effective leader. This skill will not only enhance your reputation as a good communicator but also build strong ties with your team. Other than this, through your communication style, you can inspire people and bring change.

Eleven Leadership's Principles

1. Understand Yourself and Grow

You cannot lead others or understand them when you don't know yourself as a person. So, the first thing is to know who you are, what you are good at and what you need to work on. Grow yourself by joining healthy activities or building some productive habits.

2. Be Knowledgeable in Your Role

You should know what you are doing and what is expected of you. In the same way, know your team well enough; their roles and responsibilities.

3. Take Responsibility

Be accountable for your actions. Guide your team to new heights. Instead of blaming others when things go wrong, analyze the situation, take corrective action, and move forward.

4. Make Decisions

Be a decisive decision-maker. Use sound problem-solving and planning means.

5. Lead by Example

Be exemplary. Be a role model for fellows. Set a good example for others. Show them through your actions, not just words, how to do things.

6. Respect and Care for Others

Show respect and care for people. By your gestures, show your team members that you genuinely care about them.

7. Keep Everyone Informed

Keep the team well-informed. Communicate positively with all members. Remember, communication is the key to becoming an awesome leader.

8. Encourage Responsibility

Encourage the importance of responsibility in your team. Help team members develop positive qualities that will help them do their tasks well.

9. Ensure Tasks Get Done

Ensure all tasks get done. Ensure that the team know their assigned tasks. Monitor their work as required, until it is finished. Good communication is essential for completing this responsibility.

10. Build Team Spirit

Train members as a team. Many "leaders" talk of teamwork but they add little to help build team morale. Build a proper team morale in your team. Work on building a strong sense of unity and support within your team.

11. Unlock Team Potential

Use the full capacities of your team. By boosting team spirit, you can support your team to reach its full potential.

Public Speaking Tips

Public speaking is an indispensable skill for influential leadership and beyond, but it demands confidence, consistent practice, and applying specific techniques for sharing your ideas with the audience.

The following is a list of public speaking tips to help youth become confident and influential speakers on the podium.

1. Understand Your Audience

Before you start creating your content, it is essential to deeply understand your audience. Take the time to research their demographics, interests, and preferences. Knowledge about your audience will help you select the right information and examples that are relevant to them. This is important because if you prepare well to understand your listeners, you can keep getting their attention while you present.

2. Master Your Subject Matter

You become confident when you know the topic of your presentation. Research whatever is there about your topic so you don't miss out on anything. Prepare well for your presentation, get authentic references, and use relevant stories.

People trust you more when they believe you know your subject matter more than they do. Preparation will not only make you confident but also make you able to convey your message.

3. Utilize Audio-Visual Aids Effectively

You can make your presentation more effective by using some creative audio-visual aids. But it is really important to use them as per the benefit of your presentation. If you rely on them or use them much then it would harm your overall performance. The focus of your presentation can altogether be changed and the audience can get distracted.

So, use audio-visuals effectively to provide visual appeal or show the key points of your presentation. Keep a balance between what you say and what you present through those aids. The purpose of your talk is to keep the audience attentive rather than distracting them.

4. Discuss the Audience's Perspective

Do some work on understanding the needs and interests of your audience. This is as important as you showcasing your skills and ideas while presenting. Ensure that your content provides value and relevance to them. Ask yourself, "Am I addressing the questions and concerns that matter most to my audience?" This approach ensures that you stay focused on the relevant content.

5. Create a Well-Structured Presentation

A well-organized speech or presentation is crucial for effectively delivering your message. Structure your content with a clear introduction, main points, supporting evidence, and a strong conclusion. This organization not only helps you stay focused but also guides your audience through a logical flow of information. By outlining your presentation in advance, you can ensure that each segment contributes to your overall message. If you are well-prepared for this, you will surely deliver the objective of your speech.

6. Adapt and Respond to Audience Feedback

During your presentation, remain attentive to your audience's reactions and feedback. Adjust your delivery style, pace, or content based on their responses Evaluate reactions, modify your message, and stay flexible. Act upon the audience's feedback. Avoid giving a pre-recorded address, instead, maintain flexibility to build a stronger connection with the audience.

7. Be Yourself

Audiences connect with you only when you show authenticity while speaking. Be genuine in your delivery, allowing your personality and passion to shine through. Audiences are more likely to connect with speakers who are authentic and transparent, as it creates a sense of sincerity and relatability.

8. Enhance Engagement Through Storytelling

Engage your audience by compelling stories or examples that illustrate your key points. Storytelling captures the attention of listeners and makes concepts more relatable and memorable. Share personal experiences or real-life scenarios that might relate with your audience's emotions and experiences.

9. Body Language

Your body language plays a significant role in communication. Maintain a confident posture, use gestures to address key points, and maintain eye contact with your audience. Positive body language conveys confidence, openness, and attentiveness, enhancing your credibility and connection with listeners.

10. Be Energetic from Start to Finish

Begin your presentation with a compelling opening that grabs the audience's attention. You can use an interesting statistic, provocative question, relevant quote, or a story to draw their attention. Similarly, conclude your presentation with a powerful summary or call to action that leaves a lasting impression. Strengthen your key message and inspire your audience to reflect on the insights you have shared. In conclusion, summarize your address with a powerful statement that your audience will remember forever.

Real-Life Story: Greta Thunberg

Thunberg was born in 2003 in Stockholm, Sweden. She became aware of climate change in 2011. Diagnosed with Asperger syndrome in 2014, she urged her parents to reduce their carbon footprint by adopting vegetarianism and avoiding air travel. In late 2018, she began protesting outside the Swedish parliament and delivering speeches to advocate for action against climate change. Thunberg also launched Fridays for Future, a school strike movement focused on climate action.

In August 2019, Thunberg sailed from Plymouth, UK, to New York City to attend the United Nations Climate Action Summit on September 23, 2019. At the summit, she delivered a powerful speech condemning inaction on climate change. On September 18, she also testified before a congressional hearing on climate change. Rather than delivering a prepared speech, Thunberg handed members of Congress a copy of the 2018 global warming report by the Intergovernmental Panel on climate change.

Thunberg published a collection of her climate action addresses in May 2019.

Key Takeaways

- **Solid Principles Matter:** Just like a building needs a strong foundation, effective leadership is built on core leadership values.

- **Develop Your Values:** Explore and embrace essential values for leadership, covered in detail in this section.

- **Communication is Key:** Master communication skills to inspire, influence, and effectively lead others. You've learned key techniques for doing this.

- **11 Leadership Principles:** Apply the eleven principles of leadership discussed in this section to guide your leadership journey.

- **Be a Captivating Speaker:** Enhance your public speaking skills for greater impact. Public speaking tips were provided to help you.

- **Find Inspiration:** Learn from real-life leaders like Greta Thunberg. Her story offers valuable inspiration.

Thinking Time

1. How do you plan to include service, passion, and vision in your leadership style?
2. How well do you communicate as a leader, and what are you learning to improve your communication skills?
3. Out of the eleven leadership principles we've talked about, which one do you find hardest to put into practice, and why?
4. What new public speaking tip you've learned? What challenges do you usually face when speaking in front of others?

Part 3
APPROACHES AND METHODS FOR TEEN LEADERS

Setting Goals and Time Management

"Effective time management is the key to organizing the clutter of leadership, shifting distractions into possibilities, and transforming ambitions into accomplishments."

Managing your time effectively means being organized. A typical day for a leader might involve scheduling 30-minute or one-hour blocks for meetings and discussions. It is also important for leaders to stay motivated and inspire team members to complete tasks while monitoring their progress.

Time is valuable. Leaders must make tough decisions about their workload, including prioritizing tasks, assigning resources, scheduling commitments, and managing time for various activities.

Time management is a critical skill, especially in today's technological age where gadgets and screens can be distracting, making it challenging for young leaders to stay focused on their work.

Using a **priority matrix grid** can help you organize your tasks into their suitable categories. The Eisenhower Matrix or The Priority Matrix was put forth by Dwight D. Eisenhower. This helps you in managing your tasks in order of priority.

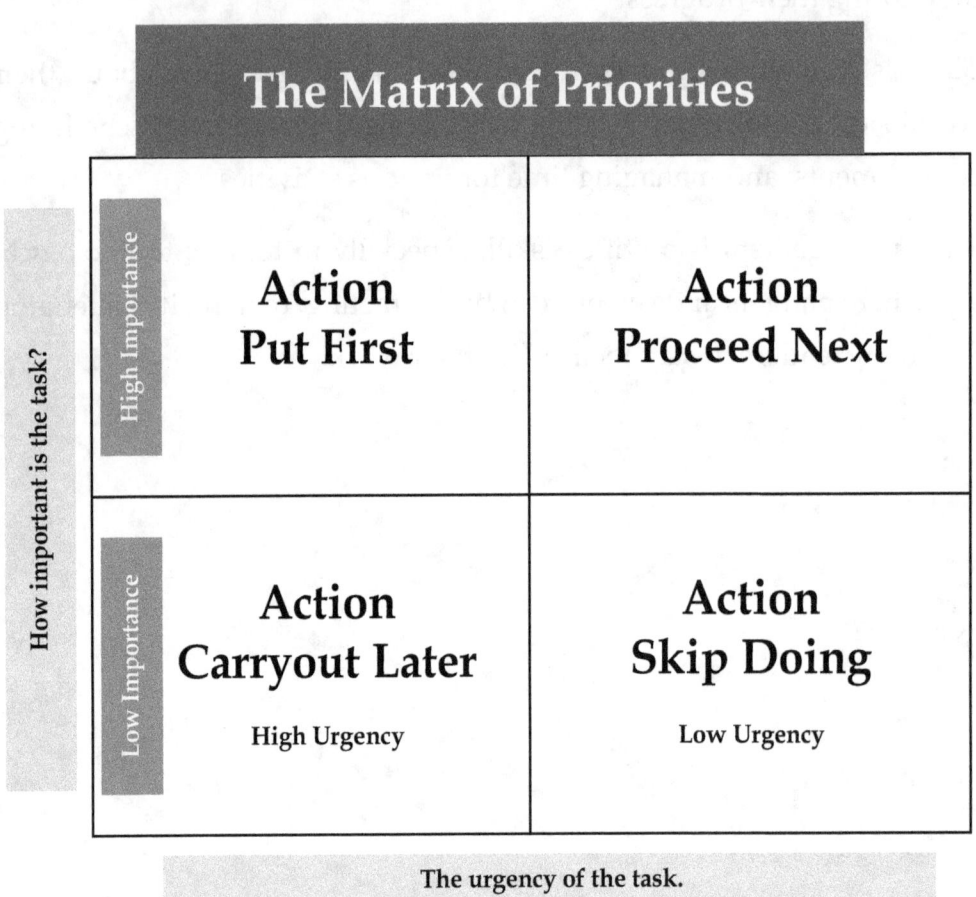

Below I'm providing you with some time management tips which you can use to create a balance between studies and your social life.

Fix Your Bed Routine

Design your schedule in such a way that you get 8-9 hours of sleep each night. This would make you fresh the next day. Also, try to wake up early so that you can finish the tasks of the day.

Fixing an earlier sleep schedule can enable early rise. Waking up early helps you deal with important tasks with a clear mind, avoiding the stress of late starts. This habit builds discipline, a key trait for leadership. Waking up early might seem tough at first, especially if you are used to staying up late. But think about the benefits, you will have more time in the morning to get things done before your day really starts. It is like getting a head start on everything you need to do!

Set Clear Goals

Setting clear, short, and long-term goals is essential for managing your time effectively. Goals give you direction and focus, helping you achieve tasks with less stress. Whether it is academic, personal, or social goals, setting them helps you prioritize your time effectively.

Setting goals is like making a roadmap for yourself. It helps you know where you are going and how to get there. For example, if you plan to write a novel in three months, break down this big task into smaller ones, and set specific time each day for writing. In this way, you can complete your task in the given timeline and won't have to rush things.

Complete One Task at a Time

If you work on a single task at one time, chances are high that you can complete it within time and in an efficient manner. Don't try to be 'Flash' and do things speedily. Doing a lot of things will only decrease your productivity and focus.

The present world will likely pressure you to do a lot of things at one time as it saves time and makes you productive. But this can effect the quality of the work you do. Quantity can significantly affect quality. Your focused attention on one thing can produce some good results.

Use Time Management Apps

You can find some useful applications for time management in your play store. These applications can help you set deadlines and avoid distractions. Also, you can cut down on your screen time and increase the efficiency of your work. You would know what is important for you to do.

These applications can even tell you how much time you have spent on social media. You can also plan your study session and mark due dates for your homework through time management apps.

Apply the Powerful Pareto Principle

The Pareto Principle was given by Vilfredo Pareto. According to this principle, 20% of what we do will determine 80% of what will happen. This understanding of the balance between action and consequences enables you to know what you have to focus on to get the desired results.

This principle is all about using your time effectively. Through this principle, you can focus on the most important thing with a huge impact and stop yourself from doing everything. For example, if you have a big project due next week, you would spend time completing it rather than using your time for other things.

Plan and Review Your Schedule

Your timetable or schedule is not just something which you make and then forget. You have to work according to it, review it weekly, and plan for the next week. Review your progress of the previous week and then make changes accordingly. If you feel like certain tasks are left unattended in the previous week, specify them in the next week and complete them on a priority basis.

Planning your schedule can save a lot of your time. You are designing how to go about life through this. This would enhance your confidence in yourself because you would be achieving more.

Balancing Studies and Leadership

You cannot ignore your studies even if you have to become a leader. This is not how it is going to work for you. You have to be a good student first and then do your responsibilities or other things side by side.

But it gets difficult for teens to keep a balance between their studies and other things. They tend to focus more on one thing. This results in poor results in one area while failure in the other.

Below I am giving you some techniques which you can use to keep a balance between your studies, hobbies, and part-time work while polishing your skills of leadership.

Strategic Leadership

When looking for leadership roles, it's good to pick ones that let you be flexible instead of just one-time tasks. This way, you can try different things and learn from them. Think about your deadlines, what you can do, and your schedule when deciding. This will help you manage your time well and make sure you're doing what you enjoy while handling your responsibilities.

Be Organized

Plan your schedule and tasks as this will help you maintain a balance between your studies and social life. Prioritize the things that need immediate action and set deadlines for your tasks. This way you will not be stressed or exhausted because you will achieve more by sticking to a routine. It is important to note that you should also include some time for breaks to relax yourself.

Be Honest

It's important, to be honest with yourself about what helps you manage your time and what doesn't. If a schedule or plan isn't working, you should change it. Learn from your experiences and be flexible to change, as this will help you find a balance that works best for you. It's also okay to say no to extra tasks if you already have so much on your plate.

Ask for Assistance

You do need people along to carry on your journey of leadership. There will be times when you want a support group. It's not a weakness if you reach out to someone. Find someone who can provide you with some helpful advice and keep you motivated towards your goals.

Manage Time

Time management is a skill which can help you achieve more than you aimed for. When you can easily tick off important things on your daily schedule, you will feel a lot of happiness inside you because the day was not wasted. Do not delay things, make a timetable if you feel like you need some motivation and a constant reminder. Paste that timetable somewhere you can see it easily.

Break down big projects into smaller and manageable tasks so that they don't look so frightening. Take time to celebrate whatever you achieve. This will keep your spirits high.

Check on Health

It is really important to live a healthy life as nothing is more important than your well-being. Don't let anything take a toll on your mental and physical health. Your productivity can be effected if you have some health issues.

Eat a balanced diet, exercise regularly and get enough sleep daily to stay fit. Developing healthy habits will keep your energy levels high and your focus will be good.

Do Not Delay Things

What needs to be done should be done on time. Only if you don't waste your time in delaying your tasks, your timelines can be met and you can achieve more. You should know what makes you delay things, either it is a distraction or being confused about how to start. Know that start is always difficult, but once you start something it gets easier because you get in the flow.

Pomodoro Method:

The Pomodoro method is a technique developed by Francesco Cirillo to get you going and avoid wasting time. This is a time-focused method which originated in the 1980s. You can use the Pomodoro technique by setting a timer for 25 minutes and then working with focus, after 25 minutes you should take a 5-minute break and then repeat.

Here is a story for you to understand how effective this technique could be:

The Power of the Pomodoro

Emma sat at her cluttered desk, overwhelmed by her homework. Her friend Jake had mentioned the Pomodoro Method, so she decided to try it. She cleared her workspace, set a goal to finish her history chapter, and wrote down distracting thoughts to address later.

Emma set a timer for 25 minutes and started working. Though it was tough at first, she soon got absorbed in her task. When the timer went off, she took a short break to stretch and get a drink.

After a few cycles of focused work and breaks, Emma finished her history assignment. Encouraged, she used the same method for her math study session and felt prepared for her test.

The Pomodoro Method helped Emma stay focused and manage her time effectively. It became her secret weapon for tackling schoolwork without feeling overwhelmed.

By implementing the above-mentioned techniques consistently, you can improve your time management skills, maintain a healthy balance between your responsibilities, and develop into a confident and effective leader in all areas of your life

Real-Life Story: Jahkil Jackson

Jahkil Jackson is from Chicago, Illinois, and is a dynamic young teen juggling different role as a pupil, tap dancer, basketball player, performer, model, and social businessman. His mission is to help the homeless in his hometown and beyond. At age 10, he's already handed over six thousand Blessing Bags filled with essential items to the needy. Remarkably, at age 8, he designed the social entrepreneurship program Project "I Am".

Jahkil Jackson is on a mission to help those in need. His project has already influenced more than forty thousand people globally and drew more attraction from donors. He is an outstanding example of persistent passion for the teens.

Formulating and Leading Effective Teams

One of the most significant strengths of a leader is creating a strong team that works well together. By encouraging strong connections within the team, a leader can increase productivity and improve employee performance. Leaders should inspire team members to collaborate and trust each other to build a strong team.

Finest Practices for Forming an Efficient Teamwork

Building strong team requires effective communication, active listening skills, and practical critical thinking approaches to help team members overcome challenges. Follow the steps below to design efficient teamwork.

- Understand the team's goals
- Facilitate communication and sentiments
- Prove yourself as a leader
- Develop strong connections between team members
- Deliver periodic evaluations

Understand the Team's Goals

Understand the team's goals before forming a team. It is crucial to define the team's overall goals and how each member will contribute to achieving them. Setting clear objectives for each team member motivates them to improve their work quality. You can also establish team goals or allow members to propose their own goals. Regular monitoring ensures they stay on track and encourages them to support and motivate each other toward achieving team goals.

Facilitate Communication and Sentiments

It is important to ask team members to share their views and appreciate their valuable ideas and opinions during brainstorming. This approach boosts their confidence and builds strong project vision within the team. Lead by example by acknowledging contributions and encouraging respect for all team members' opinions.

Prove Yourself as a Leader

Demonstrate your ability to support team members when needed. Effective leadership involves building trust with your team, promoting collaboration, and offering assistance when necessary. Recognize each team member's strengths so you can assign tasks accordingly. By showing that you are a visionary leader, you motivate the team to deliver high-quality results.

Develop Strong Connections between Team Members

Observe interactions between team members and use them when assigning tasks. For example, if you notice two team members brainstorming well together, assign them collaborative tasks. Build connections and a positive team culture through activities like team outings, team-building workshops, and group projects. These activities encourage collaboration and strengthen relationships among team members.

Motivating fellows to develop connections makes them feel more comfortable around the setting, which helps them openly communicate their ideas and create quality projects.

Deliver Periodic Evaluations

Once the team starts working together, monitor their performance and provide feedback for improvement. Conduct evaluations periodically, such as quarterly, monthly, or annually. Evaluations help you assess team performance and identify areas for improvement. Set specific goals with the team before evaluations and review progress toward those goals during evaluations. Provide guidance and strategic planning to help achieve goals, and acknowledge team members' achievements. If goals are not met, provide constructive feedback and support to help team members succeed in future evaluations.

By implementing these strategies consistently, you can enhance teamwork within your group, improve overall performance, and cultivate a positive and productive team environment.

Team-Building Activities

Building a healthy culture for your team can make them feel more passionate about collaborative work on projects. Here are some team-building activities and interaction possibilities you can use to build firmer relationships among team members:

- Volunteer days
- Celebrating individual success
- Weekly scavenger hunts
- Friendly competitions in groups

Real-Life Story: Jaylen Arnold

Jaylen Arnold is ready to change the world through his challenge. He wants to end bullying. He initiated a foundation at age eight to support and educate children who bully others.

Jaylen Arnold suffers from OCD, Tourette's syndrome (Neurological Disorder) and Aspergers Syndrome (broad spectrum Autism Disorder).

He showed symptoms of Tourette's at the age of 2 and was diagnosed at age 3. The OCD was observed by age 4, and at the age of 8, Asperger's was diagnosed.

He was called an alphabet child. Jaylen determined that rather than combating and being the victim, he could be a voice-up for other bullied kids. He established the nonprofit JCF Jaylen's Challenge Foundation educates kids across America about how they can stop bullying. Jaylen, in 2014, was cited as a "World of Children Award" honoree for his efforts in anti-bullying activism.

Key Takeaways

- **Balance It All:** Master practical time management to juggle studies, hobbies, social life, and even a part-time job.

- **Beat Procrastination:** Conquer procrastination with the Pomodoro Technique, a powerful time management tool.

- **Lead Teams to Success:** Develop essential team leadership skills:
  1. **Set Clear Goals:** Provide a clear vision to keep your team focused and motivated.
  2. **Open Communication:** Encourage open communication to foster collaboration and effective problem-solving.
  3. **Strong Team Bonds:** Build a positive and supportive team environment where everyone feels valued.
  4. **Regular Evaluation:** Track progress and adjust strategies through regular team evaluations.

Thinking Time

1. How do you manage your time to gain maximum productivity?
2. How do you see short-term and long-term goals and find them to improve your time management?
3. How did you find multitasking? Does it affect your workflow? How can you cut down distractions?
4. Why do you procrastinate? How did you find the Pomodoro method helpful?
5. What team-building activities have you been practicing, and how can you improve team collaboration?

Part 4
REAL-LIFE APPLICATIONS AND IMPACT
Creating a Global Impact

Young leadership has evolved significantly over time. The latest technologies, flexible work environments, and changing social values all play a role in shaping the future of teen leadership in both positive and negative ways. As the leaders of their teams, young leaders must adapt to these changes to achieve their goals. Today's young people will have a major impact on the economy and the future workforce.

However, young leaders face certain challenges. They are compelled by technology and culture to address complex global issues and adapt to unpredictable conditions. These challenges include:

The Ever-Changing Nature of the Contemporary Workplace

Adapting to change is essential for leadership. The ability to face and manage challenges in the workplace is a critical skill for today's young leaders. Today's work environment is always changing, so leaders need to be flexible and resilient.

Embracing Diversity, Fairness, and Inclusion

A leader should value different people. When you have people with different ethnic backgrounds in your team, you learn a lot of different things from them. This variety in leadership team brings fresh ideas which is beneficial for any team or business to grow.

Lack of Experience

A lack of experience in young leaders can often cause them problems. It's the same as sailing in unknown waters, where tides can be harsh and the journey difficult.
It could also become difficult for young leaders to gain respect from their more experienced colleagues. However, teens aiming to become leaders should polish their skills constantly so that they can improve and gain the trust of the seniors.

Social Pressure

Society expects people to behave in a certain way and leaders are no exception. Young leaders could be pressured by society to follow the already set of rules. However, fearless leaders can face this challenge effectively if they stay firm in their values. This could mean going against the norms of the society and breaking the rules.

Having said that, young leaders can always make a big difference. It takes creativity, some motivation, and a strong passion to create change in the local community or on a bigger level.

Young leaders can do this by doing the following:

Presenting Innovative Concepts and Perspectives

Young leaders should come up with new and fresh ideas and provide creative solutions to problems. They see things differently, which helps solve tough problems. By listening to young people, organizations can get new and helpful ideas.

Young people see things in new ways because they think ahead. This helps them solve difficult problems with smart ideas. By working with young people, organizations can get useful insights and fresh ideas.

Digital Proficiency

A young leader can have an edge because of familiarity with the technology. Using technology enables a young teen leader to manage the fast pace of the work. This way a lot can be done in less time. Hence, this can enhance the productivity of the work.

Influencing Public Policy

Current leadership trends have changed and young leaders need to understand that leadership doesn't only focus on managing teams but it also involves bringing political or social change.

For instance, young leaders might start projects in their communities to recycle more or use less energy. They could also work to make sure everyone gets treated fairly at school or work. These actions show how they bring new ideas and make positive changes around them.

To make a real difference, young leaders can face and tackle challenges. They can form great teams, value everyone's differences, learn from experience, and stand strong against social pressures. Their creative ideas and tech know-how can change how we work. They can also influence laws and improve how society works. With the help they need, young leaders can truly make the world better.

For you to become a leader, it is important to be a risk-taker. Be as creative as you can be, find solutions and respect your boundaries.

Your focus should be on your intellectual and professional growth. Find some role models for inspiration and get some professional teen leadership training. You should also connect with professional people and build a strong professional network. Never stop learning as learning new skills can empower you to influence others. Think of some global issues on which you can provide some of your efforts.

Below are a few suggestions and anecdotes for young people who want to address global issues.

Join Peers Abroad

With the rise of virtual learning, digital interactions, and social media, connecting with people globally has never been easier. Teens now have the ability to reach out to other teens around the world with just a few keystrokes. Various platforms, groups, live-streamed events, and webinars provide opportunities to engage in academic, extracurricular, and global discussions. These interactions help enhance your understanding of global issues and increases your interest in global issues.

Create it Experiential

When you put yourself in situations where you experience what it is like to "walk in someone else's shoes," you gain a deeper understanding of others. From a global issues perspective, the more you dive into current events, the more motivated you become to seek further knowledge and potential solutions. This type of learning helps you understand people from different backgrounds and cultures.

Look Outside the Classroom

Engaging with global concerns can be as simple as changing your educational setting. Whether it is visiting a museum, attending a global festival, or participating in a study abroad program, learning extends beyond the classroom. If you cannot travel to faraway places, you can still bring the world to you through music, films, craftwork, guest lectures, news reports, and food from different cultures. These experiences help you understand and appreciate the diversity of the world.

Stay updated with the data.

It is important to stay informed about global issues, even when the statistics are this gloomy:

- There are only twenty female heads of state globally.
- Almost one billion people suffer from hunger worldwide.
- More than one million children are affected by malnutrition.
- If the current rate of poaching and environmental destruction continues, African elephants could be extinct by 2025.

These alarming statistics provide a starting point for understanding global problems. They encourage you to ask questions like, "Why is this happening?" and "What can I do to help?" Staying informed helps you become more aware of the issues and more motivated to take action.

Develop a Sanity of Interdependence

Young people should not feel limited by borders. Just as European teens need the support of the teens in Japan, Japanese teens need the support of the American teens. Building these connections creates a sense of emotional, economic, moral, and environmental interdependence. When you understand that you are connected to teens worldwide, you are more likely to make choices that benefit many. Living in a connected world means addressing global issues is important for the well-being of everyone.

> *"Teen leaders must demonstrate the mastery and skills to deal responsibly with complex global issues. Engaging in international issues today is the initial step towards mentoring to become future global leaders."*

Real-Life Story: Gitanjali Rao

"Observe, conceptualize, research, create and communicate." These are the words of the competent teen scientist and inventor Gitanjali Rao. At fifteen years old, she has been chosen from a domain of more than five thousand competitors as TIME's annual first-ever youngster. Her extraordinary work uses technology to solve issues like polluted potable water, opioid dependence, and cyber-bullying. Her motto is to build a "global community of young innovators" to solve worldly problems. Her influential note to other youngsters: "Don't attempt to settle every problem; focus on one that thrills you." "If I can accomplish it," she said, "anyone can accomplish it."

Key Takeaways

- **Changing Leadership:** Modern technology, flexible work settings, and evolving social values have reshaped young leadership. Understand both the benefits and drawbacks of this changing landscape.

- **Challenges & Opportunities:**
    1. **Challenges:** Be prepared to navigate frequent job changes, the need for diversity and inclusion, and overcoming limited experience as a young leader.
    2. **Opportunities:** Embrace your chance to innovate, leverage technology, and even influence public policy.

- **Qualities of a Young Leader:**
    1. **Risk-Taker:** Don't be afraid to take calculated risks and learn from setbacks.
    2. **Lifelong Learner:** Always seek self-improvement and develop new skills to stay ahead.
    3. **Global Thinker:** Focus on global issues and work towards positive change on a larger scale.

- **Developing Your Leadership Potential:**
    1. **Go Global:** Connect with young leaders from diverse backgrounds to broaden your horizons.
    2. **Learn by Doing:** Seek out hands-on experiences to gain practical leadership skills.
    3. **Stay Informed:** Stay current on global challenges to identify opportunities for making a difference.

- **Real-World Inspiration:** Gitanjali Rao's story exemplifies how young leaders can innovate and make a positive impact.

Thinking Time

1. Can you adjust when things change at work or school?
2. How do you earn respect and trust when working with more experienced people?
3. What new ideas or ways of thinking have you introduced as a leader?
4. Are your tech skills helpful? Do they make your tasks easier?
5. How do you keep up with world news and use this information in what you do?

Meet the Leadership Inspo

Forget about celebrities, in this section, you will find list of the top leaders who are changing the leadership game. These are some great people who are making a real difference in the world.

Here's why we think these leaders are awesome:

R. Michael Anderson is an American who settled in England; his leadership is known across continents, helping companies do their best in Europe, Middle East, and Asia.

Marshall Goldsmith was named one of the top ten most influential corporate thinkers in 2013, the top-ranked executive coach by the Thinkers50 awards, and the top leadership thinker internationally in 2015. He is someone who makes successful people do even more amazing things! He helps leaders in developing good leaderships skills for a positive change.

Rosalind G. Brewer This woman is the most amazing Black female executive in America. She has been registered by both Forbes and Fortune magazine as a highly powerful woman.

Ken Blanchard is one of the most important leadership experts globally. He is full of creative ideas and inspirations for others. He had been on top and known as the godfather of leadership and management.

Simon Sinek is a person with vision and he thinks outside the box. He's the motivator; he prepares leaders and organizations to motivate people. He helps the people in cooperate world to unlock their true powers.

Robin Sharma is a leadership guru. He believes that everyone needs to be a leader in the recent times. He's all about dedication and taking charge of your own destiny.

Patrick Lencioni aims to build teams who are excellent in their work. He works with companies of all sizes to help them achieve success. He also delivers lectures on leadership, corporate transformation, collaboration, and business ethics.

These leaders aren't CEO's. But they are making a difference. So, get inspired and take action. It's your time to become the leader YOU want to become!

Conclusion

Being a great teen leader is not just about being perfect, it is about inspiring others and making a positive difference in their lives. The book 'Teen Leadership Unlocked' has given you many tools and strategies to help you become an amazing leader, but remember, your real adventure is just beginning!

Think of this journey like an exciting game. You will face many challenges and obstacles along the way, but if you keep going and do not give up, you will earn great rewards. These rewards are not just about winning but also about learning and growing. Keep learning new things, stay flexible, and always aim to be the best leader you can be. Be the kind of leader who inspires and motivates others with your skills and positive attitude.

Use the tips and techniques you have learned in this book to become a strong leader. You should be a flexible person, one who can adapt to change, and welcome some new ideas. You won't be successful if you don't learn. Make mistakes and learn from them.

While it is important to lead your team, it is equally important to stay kind to them and appreciate their ideas. The power and motivation you provide to your team will be doubled when they use it to make efforts for your cause.

I wish your journey of leadership to be fun. I hope you enjoy the process and become someone you're proud of. Keep learning new things and keep growing. Rest when you feel tired but just don't give up.

I believe in you and I know that you can lead, it just needs some time and practice. Work hard for your goals, stay honest to your roots, and make an impact on the world.

Before I move my pen away from this, I would like to remind you that great leaders are not just people who are successful and influential, they are people who want others to do better than them, and they are people who make others feel good.

I want you to become that leader who can bring out the best in everyone, someone who can inspire people and leave a lasting impact. Make some changes even if it's a minor one at the beginning.

Become the best leader you can think of by bringing a positive change.

> *The world needs strong leaders with a strong mindset. Why don't you become one?*

www.ingramcontent.com/pod-product-compliance
Lightning Source LLC
Chambersburg PA
CBHW082238220526
45479CB00005B/1271